THE CHILDREN'S BIBLE

Volume 4

A Golden Press / Funk & Wagnalls, Inc. Book
Published by Western Publishing Company, Inc.

Classic™ binding
R. R. Donnelley & Sons Company
patents--U.S. pending
Distributed by Funk & Wagnalls, Inc. New York
Library of Congress Catalog Card Number: 81-81439
ISBN 0-8343-0041-9 (Volume 4)
ISBN 0-8343-0037-0 (12 Volume Set)

CONTENTS

INTRODUCTION

The Hebrew people spent over forty years wending their way in the desert between Egypt and Canaan with Moses as their leader. The story of their remarkable journey is told in four books of the Bible. The story begins in the Book of Exodus, which tells us about the Ten Commandments God gave to his people on Mount Sinai. We learn more about the Hebrew people and their journey out of Egypt in the Book of Leviticus, the third book of the Bible, as well as in the fourth book of the Bible, the Book of Numbers. The story of the exodus ends in the Book of Deuteronomy, the fifth book of the Bible.

The journey to the Promised Land was difficult for the Israelites. The people often did not have enough to eat and drink. Sometimes they were chased by their enemies. Whenever the people were hungry or thirsty or discouraged, they complained to Moses. They asked Moses why God had abandoned them in the desert. God was angered by his people's failure to believe in him. God punished the people because of their mistrust in him and because he wanted to make them strong. After so many years as slaves in Egypt, they had forgotten how to live as free men and women.

Three months after they left Egypt, the Hebrews camped near a great mountain called Mount Sinai. A great cloud covered the mountain, and the Israelites watched from below as Moses went up into the cloud to meet God. God's voice sounded like thunder to the people. It was like watching a great storm and the people were afraid.

When Moses came down from the mountain he carried with him the laws that God wanted his people to obey. God wanted the people to show their love and obedience for him in everything they did. The laws that God gave his people taught them how to love one another and how to worship their Lord.

Jewish and Christian people believe that something very special happened at Sinai. The people of Israel promised God that they would obey his laws and God in return promised the people that he would always protect them and love them. These special promises that God and his people made to each other are called the covenant.

A covenant is like a treaty between two nations, or a contract between two people. In biblical times, covenants were not usually written down. The two nations or the two people who had made the covenant trusted each other. It was considered a terrible thing to break this promise.

God told the Hebrew people how he wanted them to live. He told them that if they obeyed him, he would protect them from their enemies. God made this promise only to the children of Israel. He did not make a promise like this with any other people. The nation of Israel was created when this special promise was made between God and Israel. God wanted Israel to be a special nation. He wanted the Israelites to tell all the other nations about him. After the covenant was made, the Israelites had to be very careful about what they did and how they lived. They always had to remember their promise to God.

One way in which the people of Israel showed God that they loved and respected him was by offering him sacrifices. Many times a year, the people gave God offerings of grains and meat. The meat was burned by priests on special altars.

The Bible tells us that the priests of Israel came from the tribe of Levi. The priests taught and explained the law of God to the people. If the Israelites had questions about the law, if they wanted to know how they could best live as God wanted them to live, they asked the priests. When they prayed to God, the priests of ancient Israel wore special and beautiful robes.

As the Israelites neared the land of Canaan, after all their years in the desert, they prepared to do battle with the people already living in the land. Moses had learned how to lead an army into battle while he lived in the house of the pharaoh, and under his guidance the Israelites marched on Canaan in a strict order. Each tribe had its own place in the march. Each tribe carried a banner so that Moses and the other leaders would know where all the tribes were in the battleground.

The Israelites had to fight the strong armies of the Amorites and of Bashan on the eastern borders of Canaan. These people lived in cities behind thick, well-protected walls. God helped the Israelites defeat the Amorites and the King of Bashan. Without God's help, the Israelites would have lost these battles.

God helped his chosen people and he never forgot that he had made a promise to be their protector. God made his promise with Israel because he loved his people. He promised a nation of former slaves that he would always be with them. By making the covenant with Israel, God showed the people how much he loved them. In return, he expected his people to obey his law. He wanted the people to worship him and to treat each other with respect. God was especially concerned for the poor. He told his people to take care of the poor and to be kind to strangers who came among them. Today all Jews and Christians still try to be faithful to the commandments of God.

from the
BOOK OF EXODUS
Part 2

THE TEN COMMANDMENTS

IN the third month after the children of Israel had left Egypt, they came into the desert of Sinai. They pitched their tents in the wilderness and camped there before the mountain.

Moses went up to talk to the Lord, and God called to him from the mountain, saying:

"Say to the children of Israel, 'You have seen what I did to the Egyptians, and how I carried you on eagles' wings and brought you to myself. Now if you will obey my voice and keep your agreement with me, then you shall be a special treasure to me, more than any other people. You shall be a kingdom of priests to me, and a holy nation.' These are the words you shall speak to the children of Israel."

Moses came down and called for the elders of the people, and laid before them all the words of the Lord. And the people answered together and said:

"All that the Lord has spoken, we will do."

Then Moses told the Lord what the people had said. And God was pleased and spoke to Moses, saying:

"Lo, I will come to you in a thick cloud, so that the people may hear when I speak to you, and believe you forever.

"Now go to the people and bless them today and tomorrow. Have them wash their clothes and be ready for the third day. For the third day the Lord will come down in the sight of all the people upon Mount Sinai. You shall set bounds for the people, and warn them to take care not to go up on the mountain or touch the side of it, for whoever touches the mountain shall surely be put to death. Anyone who does touch it shall be stoned or shot, whether it be beast or man. When the trumpet sounds a long blast, they shall come up to the mountain."

Moses went down from the mountain to the people, and he blessed them, and they washed their clothes. And he said to them:

"Be ready for the third day."

When the third day came, in the morning there was thunder and lightning, and a thick cloud lay upon the mountain. Then the voice of a trumpet sounded so loud that all the people in the camp trembled.

And Moses led the people out of the camp to meet with God, and they stood at the foot of the mountain.

Mount Sinai was covered with smoke, because the Lord descended on it in fire. The smoke rose up like the smoke of a furnace, and the whole mountain trembled and shook.

When the voice of the trumpet sounded long blasts, and grew louder and louder, Moses spoke, and God answered him by a voice. Then the Lord came down upon the top of Mount Sinai, and he called Moses up to the top of the mountain, and Moses went up.

And God spoke all these words, saying:

"I am the Lord your God, who

brought you out of the land of Egypt, out of the house of slavery.

"You shall have no gods other than me.

"You shall not make any sculptured image or any likeness of anything that is in heaven above, or on the earth beneath, or in the water under the earth. You shall not bow down to them nor worship them. For I, the Lord your God, am a jealous God, punishing the offspring of those who hate me, and showing mercy to thousands of those that love me and keep my commandments.

"You shall not use the name of the Lord your God carelessly.

"Remember the sabbath day, to keep it holy. Six days you shall labor and do all your work, but the seventh day is the sabbath of the Lord your God. In it you shall do no work, you, nor any member of your family and household, nor any person living with you. For in six days the Lord made heaven and earth, the sea and all that is in them, and rested the seventh day. Therefore the Lord blessed the seventh day and made it holy.

"Respect your father and your mother, so that your days may be many in the land the Lord your God gives to you.

"You shall not kill.

"You shall not commit adultery.

"You shall not steal.

"You shall not wrongly accuse your neighbor.

"You shall not envy your neighbor, nor desire to have his house, his wife, his servants, his animals, nor anything that is his."

All the people saw the thunder and lightning and heard the noise of the trumpet and saw the mountain smoke. And when they did so, they moved back and stood at a distance. And they said to Moses:

"Speak to us, and we will listen.

But do not let God speak to us, for fear that we may die."

And Moses said to the people:

"Do not fear, for God has come to test you, so that you may learn to have respect for him, so that you may do no wrong."

The people stood far off while Moses drew near to the thick darkness where the Lord was.

LAWS FOR GOVERNING THE TRIBES

And God spoke to Moses and gave him laws to govern the tribes of Israel in all their acts. And among the laws that were given were the following:

"Anyone who strikes another man and kills him must himself be put to death.

"Anyone who strikes his father or his mother shall be put to death.

"Anyone who kidnaps another, and sells him or keeps him as a slave shall be put to death.

"Anyone who curses his father or his mother shall be put to death.

"Life shall be given for life, an eye for an eye, a tooth for a tooth, burning for burning, wound for wound.

"But if a thief is killed by a person who attacks him in the act of stealing, that person shall not be punished for murder.

"If an ox gores a man or woman, and they die, then the ox shall be stoned and he shall not be eaten, but the owner of the ox shall not be charged. But if the ox was accustomed to push with his horn in time past and it has been made known to his owner and he has not kept him in, the ox shall be stoned and the owner also shall be put to death.

"If a man steals an ox or a sheep and kills it or sells it, he shall restore five oxen for an ox and four sheep for a sheep. If the animal is found in his hand alive, whether it is ox or ass or sheep, he shall restore double.

"Any man who worships any god other than the Lord shall be destroyed.

"You shall deal kindly with strangers, for you were strangers in the land of Egypt.

"You shall care for the widow and the fatherless child. If you hurt them, and they cry to the Lord, their cry shall be heard. The Lord's anger shall be great, and he will cause your own death, so that your wives shall be widows and your children fatherless.

"If you lend money to any of my people who are poor, you shall not take interest on the sum owed to you.

"You shall obey without complaint the ruler and the judges of the people."

THE ARK OF THE COVENANT

Moses came down and told the people all the words of the Lord and all his laws, and the people said:

"Everything the Lord has said, we will do."

Moses wrote down all the words of the Lord, and he arose early in the morning and built an altar to the Lord, with twelve pillars for the twelve tribes of Israel, and he sacrificed to the Lord.

Then Moses and Aaron and seventy of the elders of Israel rose up, and they saw the Lord of Israel. And God said to Moses:

"Come up to me in the mountain, and I will give you tablets of stone with the law and the commandments which I have written, so that you may teach them."

Moses and his minister Joshua rose up and before he went into the mountain of God, Moses said to the elders:

"Wait here for us. Aaron and Hur are with you: if any man has any

dispute to settle, let him go to them."

When Moses went to the mountain, a cloud covered it. The glory of the Lord was over Mount Sinai, and the cloud covered it for six days. On the seventh day God called to Moses from the cloud, and the sight of the glory of the Lord was like a raging fire on the top of the mountain to the eyes of the children of Israel.

Moses went into the cloud and up the mountain, and he was on the mountain for forty days and forty nights.

And God spoke to Moses, saying:

"Tell the people of Israel to bring me offerings. From every man who gives willingly with his heart you shall take the offering. And this is what you will receive from them: gold, silver and brass, cloths of blue, purple and scarlet, fine linen, goats' hair, rams' skins dyed red, badgers' skins and acacia wood, oil for lighting, spices for anointing and for sweet incense, onyx stones and other jewels.

"And let them make me a sanctuary so that I may live among them. They shall make it according to all that I tell you.

"They shall make me an ark of acacia wood. It shall be a chest four feet long, two feet wide and two feet high. It is to be covered with gold

inside and out, and it shall have a gold band around it. At each corner it shall have a gold ring, and through these rings shall be passed gold-covered rods of acacia wood, so that the ark may be carried.

"These rods shall remain in the rings of the ark and shall not be taken from it. And they shall put in the ark the laws I shall give you.

"They shall make also a mercy seat, a throne of pure gold, four feet long and two feet wide. At each end of the mercy seat there shall be the figure of an angel in beaten gold. And the angels shall stretch their wings upward, covering the mercy seat with them. Their faces shall look to one another and shall be inclined slightly downwards. And the mercy seat shall be put upon the ark, and in the ark shall be put the law and the commandments that I shall give you.

"And there I will meet with you, and speak to you from above the mercy seat, from between the two angels upon the ark.

"And they shall make a table of acacia wood, and cover it with gold, and put a gold band around it with gold rings at each corner. And gold-covered rods of acacia wood shall be passed through the rings, so that the table may be carried.

"And they shall make a candlestick of pure gold. Of beaten work shall the candlestick be made. Its shaft and its branches, its bowls and its flowers shall be of the same. And six branches shall come out of the sides of it, three branches out of one side, and three out of the other side. It shall all be one beaten work of pure gold. And there shall be seven lamps like this. And the tongs and the snuffers thereof shall be of pure gold. See that they are made after the pattern showed on the mountain.

"And they shall make a tabernacle, a tent lined with fine linen and with blue, purple and scarlet cloth, and covered with goats' hair cloth, rams' skins dyed red and badgers' skins.

"And the ark of the testimony, with the mercy seat upon it, shall be kept in the tabernacle and covered with a veil, a curtain of blue, purple and scarlet cloth. In front of the veil shall be kept the table. On the table shall be set showbread, twelve loaves of sacred bread shall be set there every sabbath, to be eaten by the priests.

"And the people of Israel shall

ments to consecrate him. And these are the garments which they shall make: a breastplate, an ephod, a robe an embroidered coat, a turban and a girdle.

"And they shall make the ephod of gold, of blue, of purple, of scarlet and fine twined linen, with skillful work And they shall make for the breast plate chains of pure gold. And Aaron shall bear the names of the children of Israel in the breastplate of judgmen upon his heart when he goes into the holy place, for a memorial before the Lord continually.

"And they shall make the robe al

make an altar, and set it up before the tabernacle.

"Take Aaron your brother and his sons with him from among the children of Israel, that he may minister to me in the priest's office. And you shall make holy garments for Aaron your brother, for glory and for beauty. You shall speak to all that are wisehearted, whom I have filled with the spirit of wisdom, that they make Aaron's gar-

of blue, and beneath, on the hem of it, you shall make pomegranates of blue, and of purple and of scarlet, with bells of gold between them. Aaron shall wear these garments when he ministers so that his sound may be heard both when he goes in to worship before the Lord, and when he comes out. And you shall make a plate of pure gold, and engrave upon it in the manner of a signet, HOLINESS TO THE LORD. You

hall put it on the front of the turban
and it shall be attached with a lace of
blue.

"This plate shall be at all times upon
Aaron's forehead as a token of his
ministry in order that the holy offerings
of the people of Israel may be accept-
able before the Lord.

"Aaron and his sons shall be anointed
with oil and shall be made priests, so
that they may make sacrifices to me for
the people.

"And for the sacrifice you shall take
one young bullock and two lambs
without blemish, unleavened bread, unleavened cakes tempered with oil, and
unleavened wafers anointed with oil.
You shall make them of wheat flour,
and place them in a basket, bringing it
with the bullock and the two rams.

"Then you shall bring Aaron and
his sons to the door of the tabernacle
of the congregation and wash them
with water.

"All these things shall be possible
because I have given you men of skill
and intelligence, whom I have filled
with the spirit of God. These men are
craftsmen of great experience and understanding. They are able to work in
gold, silver and brass, to cut and set
stones and to carve timber. They have
the talent to make all that I have commanded, whether the tabernacle of the
congregation, the ark of the testimony
or the mercy seat upon it.

"Speak to the people of Israel and
say: 'You shall keep my sabbaths as a
sign between me and you through all
generations. Six days may work be done
but the seventh is a day of rest, holy to
the Lord, for having made heaven and
earth in six days, the Lord rested on
the seventh.' "

And when God had finished speaking to Moses upon Mount Sinai, he
gave him two tablets of stone, the
tablets of the law and commandments,
written by the hand of the Lord.

THE MAKING OF THE GOLDEN CALF

you have brought out of the land Egypt have corrupted themselves. Th have turned aside from the way I co manded them to go. They have ma themselves a golden calf and worship it. They have made sacrifices to and have said, 'This is your go O Israel, which brought you out of t land of Egypt.' "

And God said to Moses:

"I have watched this people, a they are a stubborn people. N

W HEN the people saw that Moses was not coming down from the mountain at once, they gathered round Aaron and said to him: "Make us gods to go before us, for we do not know what has become of Moses, who brought us out of the land of Egypt."

So Aaron said to them:

"Break off the golden ear-rings which your wives and sons and daughters wear in their ears, and bring them to me."

So all the people broke off the golden ear-rings in their ears and brought them to Aaron. He took them from their hands and melted the gold and fashioned it with a tool into the shape of a calf.

"Let this be your god, O Israel, which brought you up out of the land of Egypt," they said.

When Aaron saw it, he built an altar before it. Then he made a proclamation, saying:

"Tomorrow is a feast to the Lord."

They rose up early the next morning and offered burnt offerings and brought peace offerings, and the people sat down to eat and to drink and rose up to play.

Then God said to Moses:

"Go down. For your people whom

212

therefore leave me alone, for my anger has grown hot against them, and I will destroy them and make a great nation of you alone."

But Moses pleaded with the Lord his God, saying:

"Lord, why are you angry against your people whom you have brought out of the land of Egypt by great power and with a mighty hand? Are the Egyptians to say, 'He led them out as a trick to slay them in the mountains, and to destroy them from the face of the earth?' Turn from your fierce anger against your people. Remember Abraham, Isaac, and Israel, your servants, to whom you swore by your own name that you would multiply their offspring like the stars of the heaven, and give all this land you have spoken of to their children, and that they would inherit it forever."

So the Lord repented of the evil which he planned to do to his people.

MOSES' ANGER

Then Moses turned and went down from the mountain, with the two tablets of the laws in his hand. The tablets were covered with writing on both sides and were the work of God, and the writing was the writing of God engraved upon the tablets.

When Joshua heard the noise of the people as they shouted, he said to Moses:

"There is noise of war in the camp."

"It is not the voice of those who shout for victory," Moses said, "nor those who cry in defeat, but the noise of those who sing that I hear."

As soon as he came close to the camp, he saw the calf and the dancing, and Moses' anger grew hot, and he hurled down the tablets from his hands, and they broke at the foot of the mountain.

He took the calf which they had made and burned it in the fire, and ground it to powder and sprinkled it upon the water, and made the people of Israel drink it.

And Moses said to Aaron:

"What did the people do to you that made you lead them into such great wrongdoing?"

"Do not be angry," Aaron said. "You know the people, and how they are set on mischief. They said to me, 'Make us gods which shall go before us, for we do not know what has become of Moses who led us out of the land of Egypt.' And I said to them, 'Let those who have gold break it off.' So they gave it to me. Then I cast it into the fire, and there came out this calf."

And on the following day Moses said to the people:

"You have sinned a great sin. And now I will go up to the Lord. Perhaps I can obtain forgiveness from him for the sin you have committed."

And Moses returned to the Lord and said:

"Oh, this people have sinned a great sin, and have made gods of gold. Yet, will you forgive their sin. If not, I beg you to blot me entirely out of your book."

"Whoever has sinned against me, him I blot out of my book," the Lord answered. "So go now, lead the people to the place I have told you of. My angel shall go before you. The time shall come when I shall punish the people for their sin."

THE LORD'S PUNISHMENT

And the Lord punished the people with a plague, because they had made the calf with Aaron.

And God spoke to Moses, saying:

"Depart, you and the people you have led up out of the land of Egypt, and go to the land which I promised to Abraham, to Isaac, and to Jacob for their children. I will send an angel before you to a land flowing with milk and honey. But I will not go with you myself, because you are a stubborn people."

When the people heard these words, they mourned. And not a man of them wore his ornaments.

And Moses took the holy tent and pitched it outside the camp, some way off, and called it the Tabernacle of the congregation. And whenever Moses went out into the tabernacle, all the people rose up and stood at their tent doors and followed Moses with their eyes until he was gone inside. Then the cloudy pillar descended and stood at the tabernacle door.

The Lord spoke to Moses face to face, as a man speaks to his friend. And when Moses returned to the camp, his servant Joshua remained each time in the tabernacle.

RENEWAL OF THE COVENANT

Moses bowed his head to the earth and worshiped, saying:

"If now I have found grace in your sight, O Lord, I pray you to come among us. We are a stubborn people but forgive our wrongdoing and our sin, and take us to be your people."

GOD'S PROMISE TO THE ISRAELITES

And God said:

"Behold, I will make a promise: I will do wonders for all your people such as have not been done anywhere in any nation. And all your people shall see the work of the Lord, for it is a wonderful thing that I will do.

"I will drive out before you the Amorites, the Canaanites, the Hittites, the Perizzites, the Hivites and the Jebusites. Not only must you make no agreement with the people living in the land to which you are going, but you shall destroy their altars and break their images. And you shall worship no god other than the Lord.

"You must keep all my commandments and worship me according to my laws."

Moses was with the Lord forty days and forty nights. During this time he did not eat or drink, and he wrote upon the tablets the words of the law and the ten commandments.

And when Moses came down from Mount Sinai with the two tablets in his hand, he did not know that the skin of his face shone after his encounter with God. And when Aaron and the children of Israel saw Moses, they were afraid to come near him because his face shone. Moses called to them, and Aaron and all the rulers of the congregation came to him, and Moses talked with them.

Afterwards, all the children of Israel came, and Moses told them all that the

ND God said unto Moses: "Take two tablets of stone like the first, and I will write upon these tablets the words that were on the first tablets which you broke.

"And be ready in the morning, and come up in the morning to Mount Sinai, and stand there before me at the top of the mountain. No man shall come up with you, nor must any man be seen anywhere on the mountain, nor must the flocks or herds feed anywhere near it."

So Moses cut two tablets of stone like the first. And he rose up early in the morning and went up Mount Sinai, as the Lord had commanded, taking in his hand the two tablets of stone.

And God came down in the cloud and stood with him there and said:

"I am the Lord, the Lord God, merciful and gracious, patient and with great goodness and truth. I show mercy to thousands, forgiving evil, wrongdoing and sin, but I punish the guilty even in their children and their children's children, to the third and to the fourth generation."

Lord had said to him on Mount Sinai.

Moses put a veil over his face until he had finished speaking to them. But when he went to speak to the Lord, he took the veil off. And all the children of Israel saw that the skin of Moses' face shone.

According to the commandment God had given to Moses, the children of Israel made the tabernacle. In it they placed the ark containing the tablets of stone on which were written the ten commandments and the law.

And God commanded that the tabernacle should be raised up, and he covered it with a cloud. When the cloud was taken up from over the tabernacle, the children of Israel continued their journeys. But if the cloud covered the tabernacle, they did not journey until the day that it was taken up. For the cloud of the Lord was upon the tabernacle by day, and fire was on it by night, so that all the house of Israel could see it during all their journeys.

219

from the
BOOK OF
NUMBERS

THE DEPARTURE FROM SINAI

 IT came to pass on the twentieth day of the second month of the second year after the children of Israel had left Egypt that the cloud was taken up from over the tabernacle.

So the children of Israel journeyed out of the wilderness of Sinai. The ark of the covenant of the Lord went before them, to show them where they should stop. And the cloud came to rest in the wilderness of Paran, three days' journey from Mount Sinai.

THE PEOPLE CRY OUT FOR FOOD

There the children of Israel complained again and said:

"Who shall give us food to eat? We remember the fish which we did eat freely in Egypt. We remember the cucumbers and the melons, the leeks, the onions and the garlic. But now there is nothing but this manna for us to eat."

Moses heard the people's cries, and the anger of the Lord was greatly kindled. Moses also was displeased, and he said to the Lord:

"Why have you laid the burden of this people upon me, to bring them to the land which you promised to their fathers? Where will I find food to give to all of them? For they are weeping and saying to me, 'Give us food to eat.' I cannot bear this burden alone. I pray you to kill me and save me from my misery."

And God said:

"Gather seventy men of the elders of Israel, and bring them to the tabernacle to stand there with you. I will come down and talk with you there, and I will make them share the burden of the people, so that you no longer bear it alone.

"And say to the people, 'You shall eat meat, not for one day, nor two

...ays, nor five days, nor ten days, nor ...venty days, but for a whole month, ...ntil you are bursting with it and begin ... hate it.' "

Moses answered the Lord, saying:

"The people number six hundred ...ousand, and you have said you will ...ve them meat to eat for a whole ...onth. Shall the flocks be slaughtered ... shall all the fish of the sea be gathered ... as to be enough for them?"

And God said:

"Has the Lord's power decreased at ...l? You shall see now whether my ...ord shall be carried out or not."

Moses went out and told the people the words of the Lord and gathered the seventy men of the elders. And the Lord sent forth a wind, and brought quails from the sea. He let them fall by the camp, about a day's journey on the one side and about a day's journey on the other side, all around the camp. The people went out and gathered the quails all that day and all that night and all the next day. The least that anyone gathered was about a bushel.

But even while they were eating the quails, the Lord struck the people with a terrible plague. Many of them died and were buried in that place.

THE ISRAELITES PREPARE TO ENTER CANAAN

THE Lord spoke to Moses in the wilderness of Paran saying: "Send out men to look over the land of Canaan, which I have promised to the children of Israel. Send a man from every tribe, each one to be a ruler among his people."

Moses chose twelve men, one from each of the tribes of Israel. He sent them to spy out the land of Canaan, saying to them:

"Go up into the mountains and look over the land. See what it is like, whether the people who dwell there are strong or weak, few or many. See what the land itself is like that they dwell in, whether it is good or bad. See what their cities are like, whether they live in tents or in strong buildings. See whether the land is rich or poor, whether it has wood or not, and bring back some of the fruit of the land."

Now it was the time for the first ripe grapes. So the men went out and searched the land. They came to a brook, and there they cut down a branch with a cluster of grapes on it. They carried it between them slung on a staff and they brought also some pomegranates and figs. They gave the place the name of Eschcol, meaning "a cluster of grapes," because of the grapes they had cut down there.

They searched through the land for forty days. Then they returned to Moses and Aaron and all the congregation of the children of Israel, and brought word to them and showed them the fruit of the land.

THE PEOPLE MURMUR AGAINST MOSES

And when the men returned, they said to Moses:

"We came to the land to which you sent us. It is indeed flowing with milk and honey, and this is the fruit of it. Yet the people are strong who dwell in the land, and the cities are walled and very large. We saw the children of Anak there. The Amalekites inhabit the south. The Hittites, the Jebusites and the Amorites live in the mountains, and the Canaanites have the land by the sea and along the River Jordan."

Caleb, who had been among the men sent to spy out the land, silenced the people and said:

"Let us go at once and take possession of the land, for we are strong enough to overcome it."

But the others who had gone out with him said:

"We are not able to fight those people, for they are stronger than we."

And they gave an evil report to the children of Israel concerning the land they had searched out, saying:

"The land which we went to look over is a land that eats up its inhabitants. All the people we saw in it are men of great height. We saw there giants, the sons of Anak who was descended from giants. We looked like grasshoppers by the side of them."

Then all the congregation lifted up their voices and cried. All the people wept that night. And the children of Israel murmured against Moses and Aaron, saying to them:

"Would to God that we had died in the land of Egypt, or that we had died in the wilderness! Why has the Lord brought us to this land to be killed in battle, so that our wives and children may be captured? Would it not be better for us to return to Egypt?"

And the people said to one another
"Let us choose a captain, and let u return to Egypt."

Then Caleb and Joshua, who had also been with those who had searched

then he will bring us into this land and give it to us, a land flowing with milk and honey. But do not rebel against the Lord, and do not fear the people of the land, for they have no defense. The Lord is with us. So do not fear them."

But the people threatened to stone them. And the glory of the Lord appeared in the tabernacle before all the children of Israel, and God said to Moses:

"How long will this people provoke me? How long will it be before they believe me, for all the signs which I have shown them? I will strike them with a plague. I will disinherit them and make a great nation of you alone."

MOSES ASKS GOD'S FORGIVENESS

Moses answered the Lord, saying:

"Then the Egyptians shall hear of it and they will tell the inhabitants of this land, who have heard that you are the Lord of this people. They have heard that you are seen by them face to face, that your cloud stands over them, and that you go before them by daytime in a pillar of cloud and in a pillar of fire by night. If now you kill all this people, the nations which have heard of your fame will say, 'Because the Lord was not able to bring this people into the land which he promised them, he has destroyed them in the wilderness.'

"Now I beg of you, let the Lord's power be great, even as you have spoken saying: 'The Lord is patient, and of great mercy, forgiving sin and wrongdoing.' Pardon, I beg of you, the sin of this people, according to the greatness of your mercy, as you have forgiven them from Egypt even until now."

he land, spoke to all the company of he children of Israel, saying:

"The land which we passed through o look over is an exceedingly good and. If the Lord is pleased with us,

THE MURMURERS
ARE PUNISHED

And God said to Moses:

"Because all those men who have seen my glory, and the miracles I did in Egypt and in the wilderness have not listened to my voice, they indeed shall not see the land which I promised to their fathers.

"Say to the children of Israel, 'You who have murmured against me shall die in the wilderness, but your children which you said would be captured, them I will bring to that land which you have despised. But as for you, you shall fall in this wilderness. And your children shall wander in the wilderness for forty years, one year for each of the days spent in searching out the land. For forty years I shall withhold my promise.' "

And of the men whom Moses sent to search out the land and who returned and made the congregation murmur against him by giving an evil report on the land, all except Caleb and Joshua died of a plague sent by the Lord.

Then the people rose up early in the morning and went to the top of the mountain saying:

"We are here, and will go to the place the Lord has promised, for we have sinned."

But Moses said to them:

"You must not go up the mountain. Because you turned away from the Lord, the Lord will not be with you."

Yet some of them continued and went without Moses and the ark of the covenant of the Lord, and they were struck down by the Amalekites and the Canaanites.

THE WANDERING CONTINUES

HE children of Israel continued their wandering into the desert of Sin. They stopped at Kadesh, where Miriam, the sister of Aaron, died and was buried.

Once again there was no water for the people, and they gathered themselves together against Moses and Aaron, saying:

"Would to God that we had died when our brothers died. Why have you brought the congregation of the Lord into this wilderness so that we and our cattle should die here? Why did you make us come out of Egypt to bring us to this evil place? It is no place of plenty, of figs, of vines or of pomegranates. Nor is there any water to drink."

And God said to Moses:

"Take the rod and gather the people together, you and Aaron. Speak to the rock while they look on. It shall send forth water, enough for all the people and their cattle to drink."

Moses took the rod. He and Aaron gathered the congregation together before the rock, and Moses said to them:

"Hear now, you rebels. Must we fetch water out of this rock?"

And Moses raised his hand, and struck the rock twice with his rod. The water came flowing out, and the congregation drank and their cattle drank.

But God said to Moses and Aaron:

"Because you did not believe in me, to show my power in the eyes of the children of Israel, you shall not bring this assembly to the land that I have given them."

PASSAGE THROUGH EDOM IS REFUSED

Moses sent messengers from Kadesh to the king of Edom, where the descendants of Esau lived, saying:

"We come from your kinsmen of Israel. You know all the hardship we have suffered, how the Egyptians ill-treated us and our fathers. And when we cried to the Lord, he heard us and brought us out of the land of Egypt. Now we are in Kadesh, a city on your border, and we beg you to let us pass through your country.

"We will not go through the fields or the vineyards, and we will not drink the water from your wells. We will go by the king's highway. We will not turn to the right hand or to the left until we have passed your borders."

But the king of Edom answered:

"You shall not pass through for we will come out against you with swords."

The children of Israel said to him:

"We will go by the highway, and if our cattle drink your water, then we will pay for it."

"You shall not pass through," Edom said again. And the Edomites came out against the Israelites with many people and refused to give the Israelites passage through their country.

AARON DIES

So the children of Israel turned away from Edom, and they came to Mount Hor. And the Lord spoke to Moses and Aaron on Mount Hor, saying:

"Aaron shall be gathered to his people. He shall not enter the land I have given to the children of Israel, because you rebelled against my word at the water of Meribah. Take Aaron and Eleazar his son and bring them up Mount Hor. And take from Aaron his priestly robes, and put them on Eleazar his son. Aaron shall be gathered to his people and shall die there."

Moses did as the Lord commanded. They went up on to Mount Hor while all the congregation looked on. And Moses took from Aaron his priestly robes and put them on Eleazar his son. Aaron died there at the top of the mountain, and Moses and Eleazar came down from the mountain. And all the congregation mourned for Aaron thirty days.

THE PEOPLE AGAIN REBEL

Now when the Israelites entered Canaan, they were attacked and some were taken prisoners. But later they were victorious and overcame their attackers.

In order to go around the land of Edom, the Israelites journeyed from Mount Hor by way of the Red Sea. The people were much discouraged by the land and they spoke against the Lord and against Moses, saying:

"Why have you brought us out of Egypt to die in the wilderness? For there is no bread and no water, and we hate the light bread we eat."

And the Lord sent fierce serpents among the people to bite them. And many of the people of Israel died.

So they came to Moses and said:

"We have sinned, for we have spoken against the Lord and against you. Pray to the Lord that he take the serpents away from us."

Moses prayed for the people, and God said to him:

"Make a serpent of brass and put it on a pole. And it shall be that everyone who is bitten shall live if he looks at it."

So Moses made a serpent of brass and put it on a pole. And it came to pass that if a serpent had bitten any man, when he looked at the serpent of brass, he lived.

THE AMORITES ARE DEFEATED

The wanderings of the children of Israel continued, west of Edom and along by the western edge of the land of the Moabites, until they reached the country of the Amorites. They pitched their tents in the plains of Moab, near Jericho.

And they sent messengers to Sihon, king of the Amorites, saying:

"Let us pass through your land. We will not turn into the fields or into the vineyards. We will not drink the water of the wells. But we will go by the king's highway until we pass your borders."

But Sihon would not let the people pass through his country. He gathered all his people together and went out into the wilderness against Israel. He came to Jahaz and fought against Israel.

The Israelites defeated the Amorites and took all their land and dwelt in their cities and villages.

Then they turned and went by way of Bashan. And Og, the king of Bashan, went out against them, he and all his people.

And God said to Moses:

"Fear him not. For I have put him in your hands, and all his people and his land. And you shall do to him as you did to Sihon, the king of the Amorites." So the Israelites killed Og, the king of Bashan and his sons and all his people and possessed his land.

BALAAM AND THE KING OF MOAB

BALAK, the son of Zippor, was king of the Moabites at that time, and he feared the children of Israel. For he knew of all that they had done to the Amorites. So he sent messengers to Balaam at Pethor, in the north, saying:

"There is a people come out from Egypt. They cover the whole land and are close to my country. Come therefore, I beg you, and curse this people for me, so that I may conquer them and drive them out of the land. For I know that he whom you bless is blessed, and he whom you curse is cursed."

The elders of Moab and the elders of Midian came to Balaam with Balak's message. And Balaam said to them:

"Stay here this night, and I will answer you tomorrow when the Lord has spoken to me."

The elders of Moab stayed with Balaam. And God came to Balaam and said:

"What men are these with you?"

"Balak the son of Zippor, king of Moab, has sent them to me," Balaam answered, "so that I may help him to drive out a people come from Egypt."

And God said to Balaam:

"You shall not go with them. You shall not curse the people, for they are blessed."

Balaam rose up in the morning and said to the messengers of Balak:

"Go back to your land. The Lord refuses to let me go with you."

And the elders of Moab rose and went back to Balak and told him that Balaam refused to come with them. So Balak sent other messengers, a greater number and more honorable than the first. They came to Balaam and said to him:

"We bring a message from Balak the son of Zippor: 'Let nothing prevent you from coming to me, I beg of

ou. For I will give you very great
onors. I will do whatever you tell me.
beg you then to come and curse this
eople for me.' "

Balaam answered the servants of
Balak, saying: "If Balak were to give
ne his house full of silver and gold,
cannot go beyond the word of the
ord, to do less or more. So I ask
ou also to stay here this night, so that
may know what the Lord will say
urther to me."

And God came to Balaam at night
nd said to him:

"If the men come to call you, rise up
nd go with them. But you shall do as
shall tell you."

BALAAM AND THE ANGEL

And Balaam rose up in the morning
and saddled his ass, and went with the
princes of Moab. And God was angry
because he went. So the angel of the
Lord stood in the way to oppose
him.

Now Balaam was riding upon his
ass, and his two servants were with
him, and the ass saw the angel of the
Lord standing in the way with his
sword drawn in his hand. So the ass
turned aside out of the way and went
into the field.

Balaam beat the ass, to turn her back
onto the path. But the angel of the
Lord stood in a path of the vineyards,
a wall being on both sides. When
the ass saw the angel of the Lord,
she pushed herself against a wall
and crushed Balaam's foot against
the wall. So Balaam beat the ass
again.

The angel of the Lord went further
and stood in a narrow place where
there was no way to turn either to the
right or to the left. And when the ass
saw the angel of the Lord, she fell
down under Balaam. Balaam was still
more angry, and he beat the ass with
a staff.

Then the Lord opened the mouth
of the ass, and she said to Balaam:

"What have I done to you that you
have beaten me these three times?"

Balaam said to the ass:

"Because you have mocked me. I
wish there were a sword in my hand,
for now I would kill you."

Then the ass said to Balaam: "Am
I not your ass, upon which you have
ridden ever since I became yours? Have
I ever treated you so before?"

"No," said Balaam. So God opened
Balaam's eyes and he saw the angel
of the Lord standing in the way, with
his sword drawn in his hand. And he
bowed his head and fell flat on his face.
And the angel of the Lord said to
him:

"Why have you beaten your ass
these three times? I went out to oppose
you because your way is against me.
The ass saw me and turned from me
these three times. If she had not turned
from me, I would surely have killed
you, and saved her life."

Balaam said to the angel of the
Lord:

"I have sinned, for I did not know
that you were standing in the way
against me. So now, if it displeases you,
I will go back again."

But the angel of the Lord said to
Balaam:

"Go with the men, but you shall
speak only the words that I tell you."

237

BALAAM IS BROUGHT
TO BALAK

So Balaam went with the princes of Balak. And when Balak heard that Balaam had come, he went out to meet him in a city on the farthest border of Moab, and he said to Balaam:

"Did I not urgently send for you? Why did you not come to me? Am I not able to give you great honors?"

And Balaam answered:

"You see that I have come to you, but have I now power at all to say anything? I shall speak the words that God puts into my mouth."

The next day, Balak brought Balaam up into the high places, so that he could see all the camps of the people of Israel. Then Balaam said to Balak:

"Build here seven altars and prepare seven oxen and seven rams."

Balak did as Balaam said, and together they offered on every altar a bullock and a ram. Then Balaam said to Balak:

"Stand by your burnt offering and I will go and see whether the Lord will come to me. Whatever he commands me, I will tell you."

Balaam went to the top of a hill, and God met him and said to him:

"Return to Balak, and you shall speak the words I give you."

Balaam returned to Balak, who was standing by the burnt sacrifice with all the princes of Moab, and Balaam spoke. But the words that he spoke were blessings upon Israel, and not curses.

Three times the sacrifices were offered, and each time the words God gave to Balaam were words of blessing:

"*How goodly are your tents, O Jacob,*
And your tabernacles, O Israel!
As the valleys they are spread forth,
As the gardens by the river's side,
As the sweet aloe trees
  which the Lord has planted,

And as the cedar trees beside the waters.
God brought you forth out of Egypt,
He shall eat up the nations your enemies,
And shall break their bones,
And pierce them through
  with his arrows.
Blessed is he who blesses you,
And cursed is he who curses you."

Then Balak was very angry with Balaam, and he said:

"I called you to curse my enemies, but now you have blessed them these three times. Flee then to your own country: I thought I was to give you

great honor, but the Lord has kept you back from honor."

Balaam answered:

"Did I not say to the messengers you sent to me, 'If Balak were to give me his house full of silver and gold, I cannot go beyond the commandment of the Lord, to do either good or bad; but I will speak as the Lord tells me?' And now I go back to my people, but before I go I will tell you what this nation shall do to your nation in time to come."

And Balaam made this prophecy:

"There shall come a star out of Jacob,
And a sceptre shall rise out of Israel,
And shall strike the land of Moab,
And destroy all the children of
  Sheth.
Edom shall be conquered,
And Israel shall do valiantly.
Out of Jacob shall come a man
  of great power,
And he shall destroy all that remains
  of the city."

Then Balaam rose and returned to his own country, and Balak also went his way.

from the
BOOK OF
DEUTERONOMY

MOSES' LAST WORDS TO HIS PEOPLE

HE forty years of wandering were coming to an end and Moses spoke to the people of Israel, saying:

"Now these are the commandments, the statutes, and the judgments which the Lord your God commanded me to teach you, so that you might do them in the land which you go to possess. Hear, therefore, O Israel, and be sure to do it, that all may be well with you and that you may increase mightily, as the Lord God of your fathers promised you, in the land flowing with milk and honey.

"The Lord our God is one Lord, and you shall love the Lord your God with all your heart and with all your soul and with all your might.

"And these words which I command you this day shall be in your heart, and you shall teach them carefully to your children. You shall talk of them when you sit in your house, and when you walk along the road, and when you lie down, and when you rise up.

"You shall bind them as a sign on your hand, and they shall be as frontlets between your eyes. And you shall write them upon the posts of your house, and on your gates.

"You shall fear the Lord your God, and serve him, and shall swear by his name. You shall not go after other gods, the gods of the people who are round about you, lest the anger of the Lord your God be kindled against you and destroy you from the face of the earth.

"And it shall come to pass when your son asks you in time to come, 'What do the testimonies and the statutes and the judgments mean?' that you shall say to your son, 'We were Pharaoh's servants in

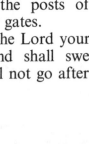

242

gypt, and the Lord brought us out f Egypt with a mighty hand, and the ord showed signs and wonders, great nd grievous, against Egypt, against haraoh, and against all his household, efore our eyes.

" 'And he brought us out from here that he might bring us into and ive us the land which he promised to our fathers. And the Lord commanded us to obey all these statutes: to fear the Lord our God, for our good always, that he might preserve us alive as it is this day. And it shall be our righteousness if we observe all these commandments before the Lord our God, as he has commanded us.'

"All these commandments I have given you, so that you may live, and multiply, and go in to possess the land which the Lord promised to your fathers. And you shall remember all the way which the Lord your God led you for these forty years in the wilderness, to humble you and to test you, to know what was in your hearts, whether you would keep his commandments or not. And he humbled you, and caused you to go hungry, and fed you with manna, which neither you nor your fathers had ever seen before, so that he might make you know that man does not live by bread only, but by every word that comes from the mouth of God.

"You shall also remember that as a father punishes his son, so the Lord your God punishes you. Therefore you shall keep the commandments of the Lord your God, to walk in his ways and to stand in awe of him.

"For the Lord your God is bringing you to a good land, a land of brooks and water, of fountains and wells that spring out of valleys and hills; a land of wheat and barley, of vines, fig trees and pomegranates; a land of oil-olives and honey; a land where you shall have plenty of bread to eat, where you shall not lack any thing; a land whose stones are iron and out of whose hills you may dig brass.

"When you have eaten and are full, then you shall bless the Lord your God, and give him thanks for the good land he has given you.

"Beware that you forget not the Lord your God; that you keep his commandments, his judgments and his laws which I have given you.

"Take care that when you have eaten and are full, and have built fine houses to live in, and when your herds and flocks multiply, and your silver and gold and all that you have has increased, that you do not become proud and forget the Lord your God who brought you forth out of the land of Egypt, from the house of slavery; who led you through that great and terrible wilderness, where there were fierce serpents, and scorpions, and drought, and not a drop of water. Do not forget the Lord who brought you water out of the rock of flint, who fed you in the wilderness with manna so that he might humble you and test you. Take care that you do not say in your hearts, 'My power and the strength of my hand have got me these riches.'

"But you shall remember the Lord your God, for it is he who makes you able to get riches, so that he may keep the promise which he made to your fathers, as he does today.

"And it shall be, if you ever forget the Lord your God, and follow other gods and worship them, you shall indeed perish. You shall perish as the nations which the Lord has destroyed before your eyes, because you would not obey the voice of the Lord your God."

THE LORD IS GOING
BEFORE YOU

And Moses continued, saying:

"Hear, O Israel: You are to pass over Jordan, to go in to possess nations greater and stronger than you. Understand therefore that the Lord your God is going over before, that he shall destroy them as a raging fire, and he shall bring them down before you. So you shall drive them out and

destroy them quickly, as the Lord ha said.

"Do not say in your heart, after the Lord your God has driven them before you, 'It is because of my own goodness that the Lord has brought me to possess this land.' It is because of the wickedness of these nations that the Lord is driving them out before you. It is not because of your own goodness, or the upright-

ness of your heart, but because of their wickedness, and so that the Lord your God may keep the promise which he made to your fathers, Abraham, Isaac, and Jacob.

"Therefore, as I have said, you shall keep these words of mine in your heart and in your soul, and you shall teach them to your children, speaking of them at all times: when you are in your houses, and when you are making a journey, when you lie down to sleep, and when you rise in the morning. You shall write them on the doorways of your houses and on your gates, so that you may live long, and so that your children may live long, in the land which the Lord promised your fathers.

"And it shall come to pass, if you listen diligently to the voice of the Lord your God and observe and do all his commandments, that the Lord your God will set you on high above all the nations of the earth. And all these blessings shall come to you, if you listen to the voice of the Lord your God.

244

"Blessed you shall be in the city,
and blessed shall you be in the field.
Blessed shall be the fruit of your body,
and the fruit of your ground,
and the fruit of your cattle,
and the flocks of your sheep
Blessed you shall be when you come in
and blessed shall you be when you go out.

"But it shall come to pass, if you ll not listen to the voice of the Lord ur God and observe and do all his

mmandments, that all these curses all come upon you:

"Cursed you shall be in the city,
and cursed shall you be in the field.
Cursed shall be the fruit of your body,
and the fruit of your land,
and the flocks of your sheep.
Cursed you shall be when you come in,
and cursed shall you be when you go out.

"The Lord shall strike you with a rning fever, and with the sword and ith mildew, and these shall plague you til you perish. The Lord shall make e rain of your land powder and dust. rom heaven it shall come down upon u until you are destroyed.

"The Lord shall bring a nation ainst you from afar, from the end of e earth, as swift as the eagle flies, a tion whose tongue you shall not derstand, a nation of fierce appear- ce which shall show no favor to e old or young. It shall besiege you all your gates, until your high walls me down which you trusted. And it all besiege you throughout all the

land which the Lord your God has given you.

"If you will not do all the words of this law that are written in this book, the Lord shall scatter you among all people, from one end of the earth to the other. And there you shall serve other gods which neither you nor your fathers have known, gods of wood and stone. And among these nations you shall find no ease, nor shall the sole of your foot have rest, but the Lord shall give you there a trembling heart, and failing of eyes and sorrow of mind.

"Your life shall hang in doubt before you and you shall fear day and night and shall have no assurance for your life. In the morning you shall say, 'Would to God it were evening!' And at evening you shall say, 'Would to God it were morning!' And the Lord shall bring you back into Egypt in ships, and there you shall be offered for sale as slaves, but no man shall buy you.

"And it shall come to pass when all these things have happened to you, the blessing and the curse, you shall return to the Lord your God and shall obey his voice according to all that I command you this day, you and your children with all your heart and with all your soul. Then the Lord your God will have compassion upon you and will return and gather you from all nations where he has scattered you. And the Lord will bring you into the land which your fathers possessed, and you shall possess it. And he will do you good and multiply you more than your fathers.

"See, I have set before you this day life and good, and death and evil. I call heaven and earth to record this day against you, that I have set before you life and death, blessing and cursing. Therefore choose life so both you and your offspring may live and love the Lord your God."

THE DEATH
OF MOSES

ND Moses went and spoke these words to all Israel. Then he said to them:

"I am a hundred and twenty years old this day. I can no longer go out and come in. Also the Lord has said to me, 'You shall not go over the Jordan.' Joshua, he shall go over before you, as the Lord has said."

And Moses called Joshua and said to him in the sight of all Israel:

"Be strong and of good courage. For you must go with this people into the land which the Lord has promised their fathers. And you shall cause them to inherit it."

Then God said to Moses:

"Behold, you shall sleep with your fathers, and this people will rise up and will forsake me and break the agreement which I have made with them. Take down therefore this song and teach it to the people of Israel that they may learn it by heart. It shall be a witness for me against them. Then I will hide my face from them, when they have turned to other gods. Many evils and troubles shall plague them."

So Moses spoke in the ears of all the congregation of Israel the words of this song:

"Give ear, O you heavens, and I will speak
    and hear, O earth, the words of my mouth

My doctrine shall drop as the rain,
    my speech shall distill as the dew,
        as the small rain upon the tender herb
        and as the showers upon the grass.

For I will proclaim the name of the Lord

He is the Rock, his work is perfect,
    for all his ways are just.

A God of truth and without iniquity,
    just and right is he.

Remember the days of old,
    consider the years of many generations.

Ask your father and he will show you,
    your elders, and they will tell you.

For the Lord's portion is his people,
Jacob is his inheritance.

He found him in a desert land,
and in the waste of the howling wilderness.

He led him about, he instructed him,
he kept him as the apple of his eye.

As an eagle stirs up her nest,
flutters over her young,
spreads out her wings, takes them,
carries them on her wings.

So the Lord alone did lead him,
and there was no strange god with him.

He made him ride on the high places
of the earth, that he might eat
the increase of the fields,
and he made him suck honey out of the rock,
and oil out of the flinty rock.

Of the Rock that begot you
you are unmindful,
and have forgotten God who formed you.

The Lord saw it, and spurned them,
because of the provocation
of his children.

And he said, I will hide my face from them,
I will see what their end shall be.

For they are a very wayward generation,
children in whom there is no faith.

For they are a nation void of counsel,
nor is there any understanding in them.

O that they were wise and understood this,
and would see their ending!"

247

And after Moses came and spoke all the words of this song in the ears of the people, God spoke to him, the same day, saying:

"Go up on to Mount Nebo, in the land of Moab near Jericho. And look at the land of Canaan which I am giving to the children of Israel. And die on the mount and be gathered to your people, as Aaron your brother died on Mount Hor and was gathered to his people. You shall see the land before you, but you shall not go into this land which I have promised to the children of Israel."

So Moses went up from the plains of Moab into the mountain of Nebo, to the peak of Pisgah, by Jericho. And the Lord showed him all the land he was giving to each of the tribes of Israel. And the Lord spoke to him, saying:

"This is the land which I promised to Abraham, to Isaac, and to Jacob, saying I would give it to their children. I have allowed you to see it with your own eyes, but you shall not go over there."

So Moses the servant of the Lord died there in the land of Moab, according to the word of the Lord. He was buried in a valley in the land of Moab, near Bethpeor, but no man knows to this day where his grave lies.

And Moses was a hundred and twenty years old when he died. But his eye was not dimmed, and his strength had not failed him.

The children of Israel wept for Moses in the plains of Moab for thirty days. Then the days of weeping and mourning for Moses were over.

And Joshua, the son of Nun, was full of the spirit of wisdom, for Moses had laid his hands on him and blessed him. And the children of Israel listened to him and did as the Lord commanded.

Never again in Israel was there a prophet like Moses, whom the Lord knew face to face, and who did all the signs and wonders which the Lord sent him to do to Pharaoh in the land of Egypt. Such was the wondrous power which Moses showed in the sight of all Israel.

ILLUSTRATED GLOSSARY

Acacia wood (p. 208)

The wood of the acacia tree was valued because it is sweet-smelling. The acacia was common in dry areas of the Bible lands. From its Hebrew name, *seneh*, comes the word Sinai: the dry peninsula where acacia trees grew in large numbers.

Aloe tree (p. 238)

This tree was used for making a pleasant-smelling gum called aloes. Mixed with cinnamon and myrrh, aloes was used to perfume clothing and bedding.

The succulent plants we now call aloes are not related to the aloes of the Old Testament.

Altar (p. 206)

An altar in biblical times was a place where sacrifices were offered to God. (See Sacrifice.) Early altars were simply piles of stones. Animal sacrifices were burned on top of the stones.

An altar was usually built outdoors on a hill. Many years later, when the beautiful Temple of Solomon was built, the Altar of Burnt Offerings was built so high that its top could be reached only by steps.

There was another kind of altar in Hebrew places of worship—the Altar of Incense. This was a gold–topped table on which incense (see Incense) was burned.

Amorites (p. 218)

The Amorites were a Semitic tri[be] from Mesopotamia. Amorites on[ce] ruled in Babylon, and later ruled in A[s]syria. They were also kings in Jerich[o,] a city in Canaan.

Anointing (p. 208)

Anything that was to be devoted [to] God's service was rubbed with a mi[x]ture of olive oil and fragrant spices in [a] religious ceremony called anointin[g.] Priests were also anointed before the[y] took up the service of the Lord.

Bashan (p. 233)

Bashan, an area east of the Sea [of] Galilee, was known for its good pa[s]ture land and for the fine cattle raise[d] there. Psalm 22 talks about the "stro[ng] bulls of Bashan." In Ezekiel, we rea[d] "of rams, of lambs, and of goats, [of] bulls, all of them fat animals [of] Bashan."

Breastplate (p. 210)

Over the ephod (see Ephod) an Isr[a]elite priest wore a bejeweled breas[t]plate. The breastplate was a square [of] fabric that hung from gold chains an[d] as attached to the shoulders of the ephod. Four rows of jewels, with three jewels in each row, adorned the breastplate. The jewels were sardius, topaz, carbuncle, emerald, sapphire, diamond, jacinth, agate, amethyst, beryl, onyx, and jasper. Each of the twelve stones represented one of the twelve Tribes of Israel and the name of a tribe was engraved on each stone.

Edom (p. 231)

Edom was a land south of the Dead Sea, in what is now the country of Jordan. The people of Edom, the Edomites, were descended from Esau, the twin brother of the patriarch Jacob, and were miners and traders. Although they were Semites and related to the Israelites, they would not allow Moses to lead his followers through the land of Edom on their way to the Promised Land. They probably feared such a great number of strong-looking strangers.

Ephod (p. 210)

The priests of the Israelites wore an outer garment called an ephod when they offered a sacrifice. It was sleeveless, reached to about the knees, and was beautifully embroidered in colorful threads. On each shoulder there was an onyx (see Onyx) on which the names of six of the sons of Israel (Jacob) were engraved.

Frontlet (p. 242)

A frontlet is a band worn on the forehead. Before his death, Moses preached to his people about loving God, and he told them to wear his words on the hand and as a frontlet. Hebrew men obeyed by wearing phylacteries, small boxes containing Moses' words, strapped to their foreheads and left arms when they prayed. Some of Moses' words that were included are: "Hear, O Israel: The Lord our God is one Lord; and you shall love the Lord your God with all your heart and with all your soul, and with all your might."

Grapes (p. 224)

Grapes grew well, and still do, in the sunny climate of the Holy Land. But the farmer who wanted a rich harvest of grapes had to guard his plants, since foxes and jackals would raid the grapevines.

Frequently an owner built a booth in his grape fields where a watchman stood to guard the harvest. A brick wall also surrounded the vineyard for added protection.

The ripe grapes were harvested in baskets in late summer or early fall, and piled into big stone vats. Then barefooted people trod on the grapes, pressing out the juice, which was later made into wine.

Some grapes were made into raisins. The ripe grapes were spread on the flat roof of the vineyard owner's house and dried in the sun.

Hittites (p. 218)

The Hittites were people who came from what is now Turkey. They were not Semites. At one time the Hittites ruled Syria and had great influence over the other countries in the East, with whom they frequently fought.

Hivites (p. 218)

The Hivites were a small tribe of non-Semitic people. They lived in Canaan, west of the Jordan River, in an area that lay around the town of Shechem.

Incense (p. 208)

Incense is a powder made of spices, musk, and aromatic plant parts. When it is burned, incense produces a fragrant smoke.

Moses told his people that every morning they were to burn incense made from spices, frankincense, and salt on the Altar of Incense (see Altar) as an honor to the Lord. When this powder was dropped on hot coals, a sweet-smelling cloud rose from it.

Jebusites (p. 218)

The Jebusites were a small tribe that lived in and around what later became Jerusalem.

The Jordan River (p. 226)

The Jordan River runs from north to south in the Holy Land. It begins on Mount Hermon at the northern tip of the country, near the city of Dan. Mount Hermon is nine thousand feet high and is always covered with snow. As the snow melts it runs down the mountainside, joining with the waters of mountain springs, to form the beginnings of the Jordan River.

The river runs swiftly downhill and widens to form the small Lake Hula. From there it races on until it forms the fourteen-mile-long Sea of Galilee, seven hundred feet below sea level.

From out of the Sea of Galilee the river flows through a very deep valley and comes to an end at the Dead Sea, thirteen hundred feet below sea level.

Kadesh (p. 229)

Moses and the Israelites stayed at the oasis Kadesh for thirty-eight years. Known also as Kadesh-Barnea, this oasis in the Sinai desert had two fine springs that supplied water all year long. The Israelites probably did some farming during the time they were at Kadesh-Barnea.

King's Highway (p. 231)

The king's highway was a caravan road that passed through many important cities. The road began at Ezion-Geber on the northern tip of the Gulf of Aqaba, and ran north through the lands of the Edomites, Moabites, Amorites, and Ammonites. From there it went through Gilead and Bashan.

Mount Nebo (p. 248)

Mount Nebo is located ten miles east of the northern tip of the Dead Sea. From Mount Nebo, Moses could look across the Jordan River to Canaan, the Promised Land.

Onyx (p. 208)

Onyx is a semiprecious stone banded with different colors, such as black and white, or brown and white. It is sometimes used in jewelry.

Pomegranate (p. 210)

Pomegranate fruits look somewhat like apples, but have many red seeds in their pulpy insides. The pomegranate seeds are very juicy, and the people in Bible lands liked to drink the juice.

Sacrifice (p. 206)

A sacrifice was an offering made to God. The Hebrews made sacrifices to thank God for his goodness to them, and to show that everything they owned and enjoyed came from the Lord. The sacrifice was something valued by the person offering it, such as a lamb, bird, or calf.

After the animal was killed, it was completely drained of blood. Then parts of the animal were burned on an altar. Along with the burnt offering, other foods, such as oil, flour, or wheat, were sacrificed.

Scorpion (p. 244)

The scorpion is a pale stinging insectlike animal that may measure eight inches long. Its sting can be quite painful to the victim, but is seldom fatal. Scorpions are found all over the Holy Land. They hide in rocks during the day, and come out at night to hunt for prey like insects and spiders.

Showbread (p. 210)

Unleavened bread that was dedicated to the Lord was called showbread. Twelve loaves of showbread, made of fine wheat, were set on a table outside the place where the Ark of the Covenant was kept. They were arranged in two rows of six each, as an offering of thanks to the Lord. After the showbread was replaced by fresh loaves, the priests ate the old loaves.

Tablets of stone (p. 211)

During biblical times, writing was carved into slabs of stone, or written with pen and ink on paper made of papyrus. God gave Moses large, flat pieces of stone into which the words of the Ten Commandments were cut.

After the Ark of the Covenant was erected, the two sacred tablets were kept in it. The Ark and its contents were thought to be so holy that only Levites were allowed to touch it. Later, the Ark and the tablets were kept in King Solomon's Temple in Jerusalem, where they were stolen by the Romans. They later disappeared.

Turban (p. 210)

An Israelite priest wore a soft head-covering, called a turban, made of fine linen. It was fastened to his head with a band adorned with a pure gold plate. On this plate was engraved "Holiness to the Lord." The plate was attached to the band by blue laces.

Twelve Tribes of Israel (p. 206)

The people who descended from the twelve sons of Israel (Jacob) were called the Twelve Tribes of Israel. The names of the sons and of the tribes they fathered were: Reuben, Simeon, Levi, Judah, Issachar, Zebulun, Dan, Naphtali, Gad, Asher, Joseph, and Benjamin. Sometimes the Bible names Joseph's sons Manasseh and Ephraim as tribal leaders because they inherited Joseph's birthright. Often the Levites, the priestly tribe, are omitted because they had no land.